YOUNG ARTIST SERIES

LEARN TO DRAW... 3D ILLUSIONS and MORE!

Illustrated by Kerren Barbas Steckler

Designed by Heather Zschock

PETER PAUPER PRESS, INC.
Rye Brook, New York

For Emily, Audrey, and Jake

PETER PAUPER PRESS

In 1928, at the age of twenty-two, Peter Beilenson began printing books on a small press in the basement of his parents' home in Larchmont, New York. Peter—and later, his wife, Edna—sought to create fine books that sold at "prices even a pauper could afford."

Today, still family owned and operated, Peter Pauper Press continues to honor our founders' legacy of quality, value, and fun for big kids and small kids alike.

Illustrations copyright © 2020 Kerren Barbas Steckler
Designed by Heather Zschock

Copyright © 2020
Peter Pauper Press, Inc.
Manufactured for Peter Pauper Press, Inc.
3 International Drive
Rye Brook, NY 10573 USA
All rights reserved
ISBN 978-1-4413-3503-6
Printed in China

Published in the United Kingdom and Europe by
Peter Pauper Press, Inc.
c/o White Pebble International
Units 2-3, Spring Business Park
Stanbridge Road
Havant, Hampshire PO9 2GJ, UK

Visit us at www.peterpauper.com

HEY, ARTISTS!

Are you ready to take your drawings . . .

TO THE NEXT DIMENSION?

It's easier than you think!

To draw any of the illusions in this book, just follow the numbered steps. All you'll need is a **regular pencil** with an **eraser**. You can draw on the practice page following the instructions, or on a separate piece of paper. Each new step is shown in red. Draw blue lines more lightly, and if you see a dashed line (- - -), erase it. Lastly, **shade** your drawings in light, medium, and dark gray as shown. Shading makes your drawings look 3D by imitating the shadows cast by real objects.

 **First,** pressing very lightly with your pencil, shade an area light gray.

 **Then,** using medium pressure with your pencil, shade an area medium gray.

 **Then,** pressing more heavily (but not too heavily) with your pencil, shade an area dark gray.

Once you get the hang of a drawing, try adding color. You're on your way to creating 3D masterpieces!

GET READY! GET SET! DRAW!

1.
2.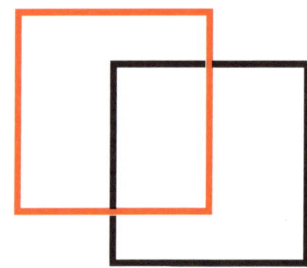
3.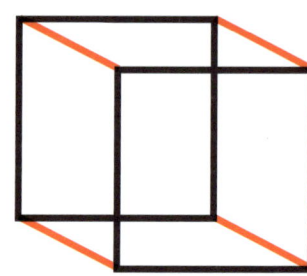

Follow the steps in red to draw a cube.

4.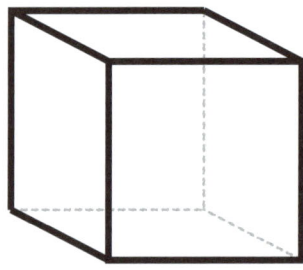
5.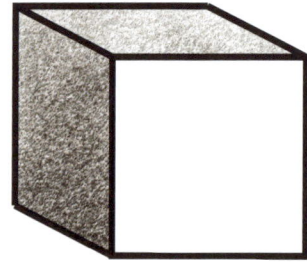
6.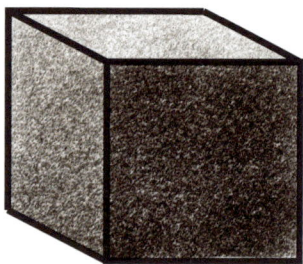

Erase the dashed lines.

Shade the top of the box light gray. Shade the side of the box medium gray.

Shade the front of the box dark gray.

1.
2.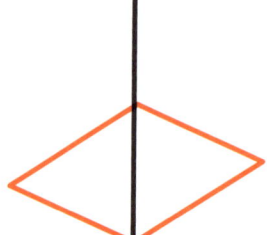
3.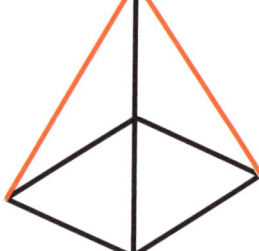

Follow the steps in red to draw a pyramid.

4.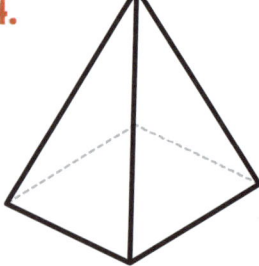
5.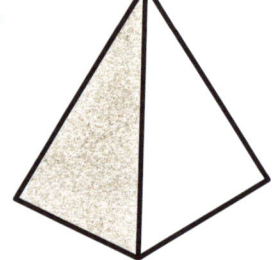
6.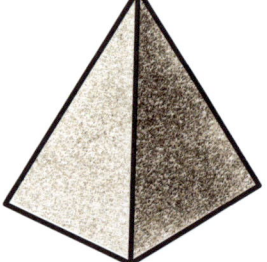

Erase the dashed lines.

Shade one side light gray.

Shade the other side dark gray.

· PRACTICE PAGE ·

Start by following steps 1–3 on the previous page to draw a pyramid.

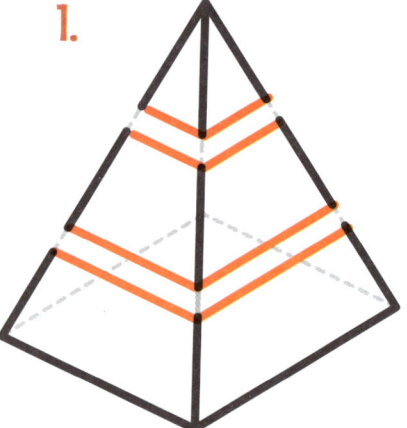
1.
Erase the dashed lines.

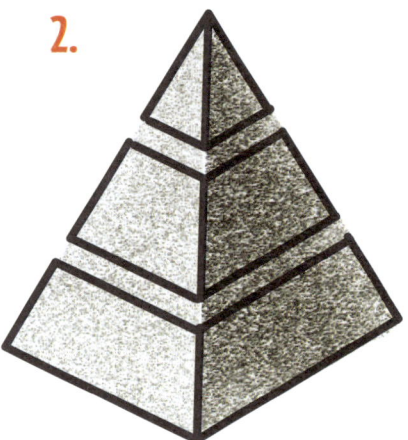
2.
Shade one side light gray and one side medium gray.

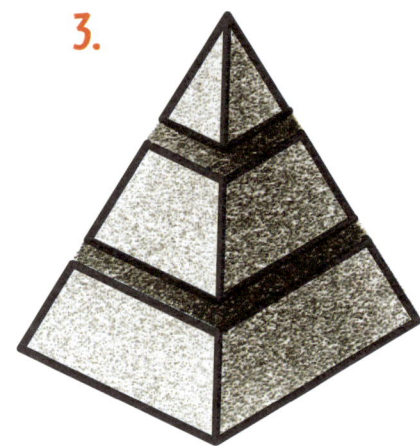
3.
Shade dark gray as shown.

Start by following steps 1–3 on the previous page to draw a pyramid.

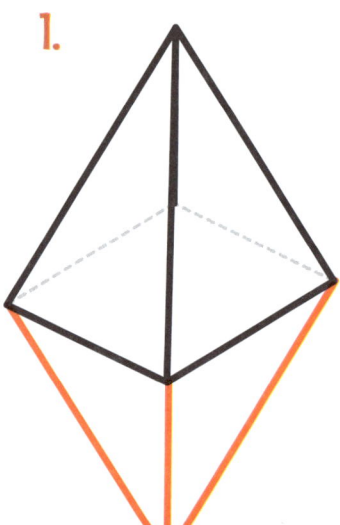
1.
Erase the dashed lines.

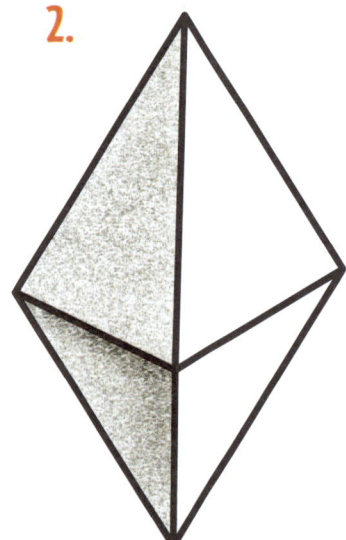
2.
Shade the left side light gray. Add a little medium gray on the bottom half.

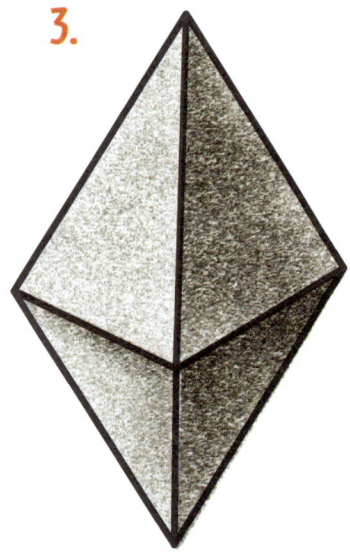
3.
Shade the top of the right side medium gray, and the bottom dark gray.

• PRACTICE PAGE •

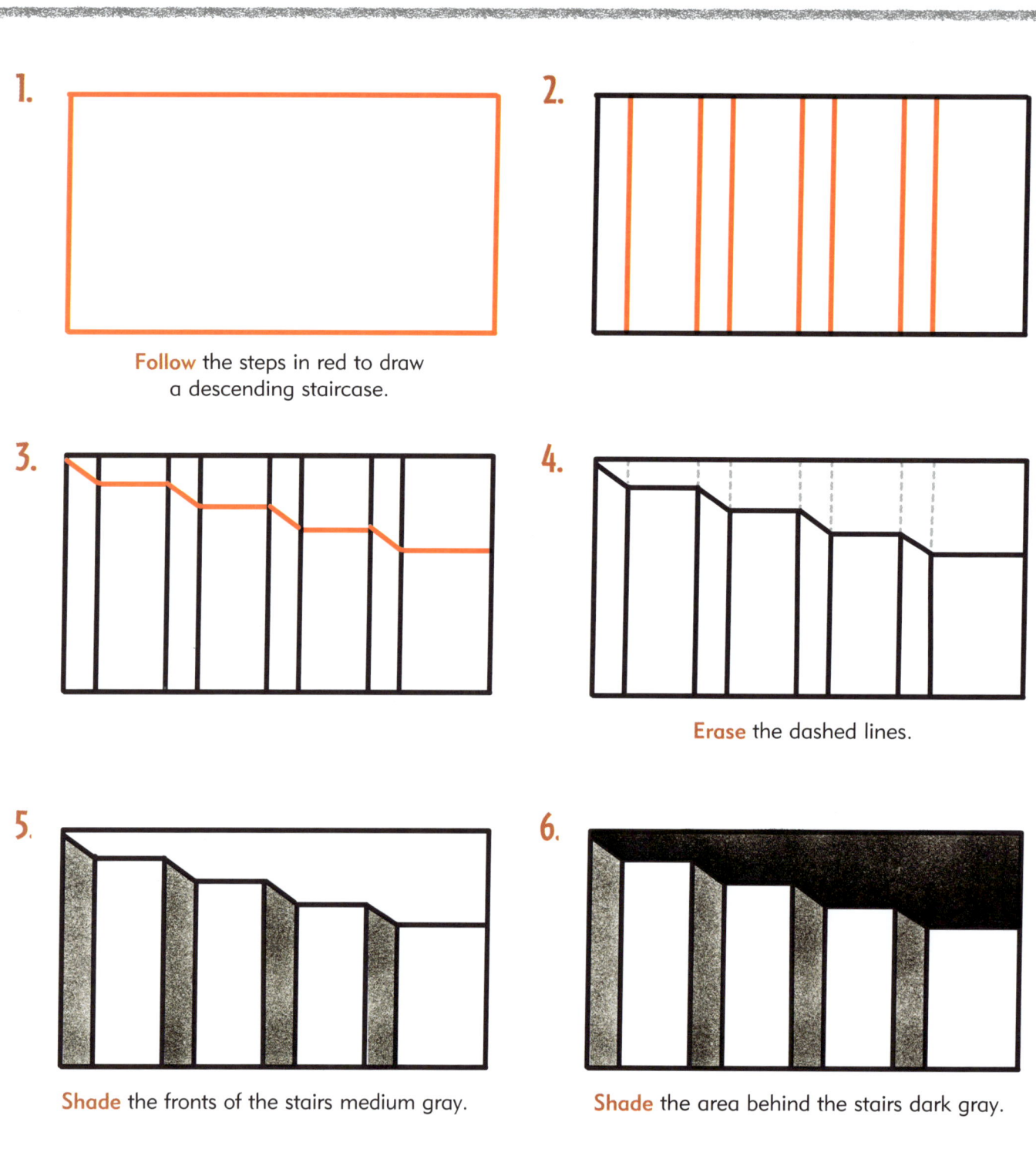

• PRACTICE PAGE •

1.

Follow the steps in red to draw a striped hole in the paper.

2.

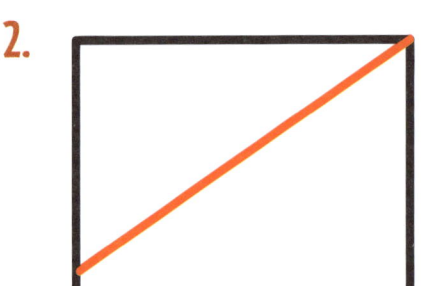

3.

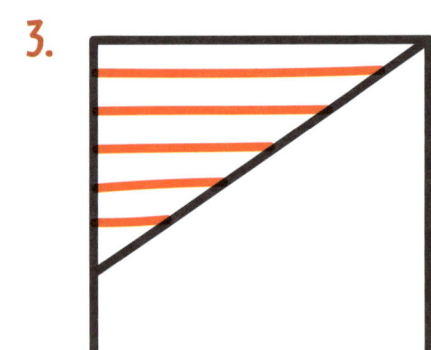

4.

5.

Shade every other stripe medium gray.

6.

Shade the gray stripes in the lower part of the box darker gray.

7.

Shade the white stripes in the lower part medium gray.

Extra tip! Tilt your drawing and notice how the perspective changes.

• PRACTICE PAGE •

1.

Follow the steps in red to draw a floating cube.

2.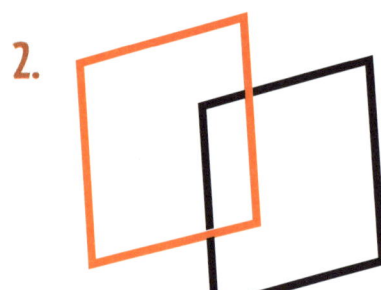

3.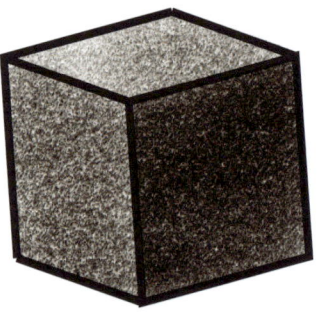

4.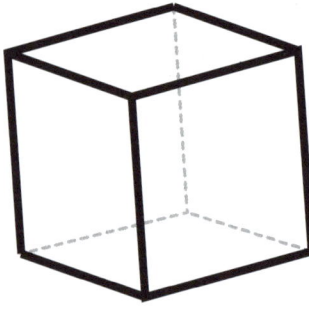

Erase the dashed lines.

5.

Shade the top and side of the cube medium gray.

6.

Shade the front of the cube and the shadow beneath it dark gray.

1.

Follow the steps in red to draw a flat-sided prism.

2.

3.

4.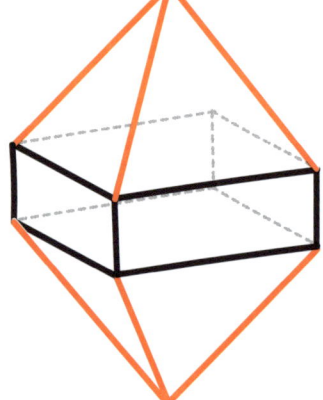

Erase the dashed lines.

5.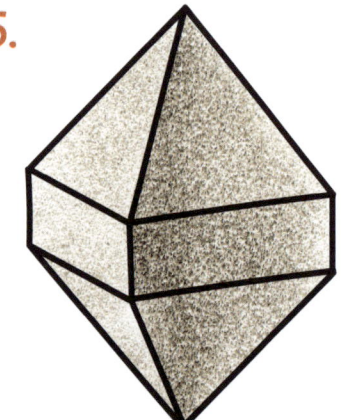

Shade the left side of the prism light gray. Shade the front medium gray.

6.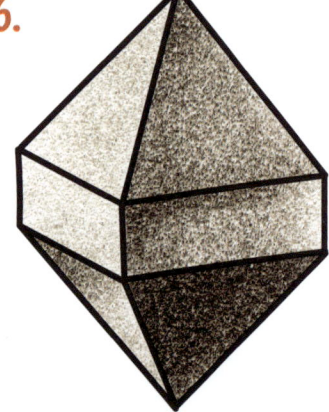

Shade dark gray around the corners and bottom of the prism as shown.

• PRACTICE PAGE •

1.

To begin, lightly draw the guidelines shown in blue.

2.

Follow the steps in red to draw a 3D shooting star. Erase the dashed line.

3.

4.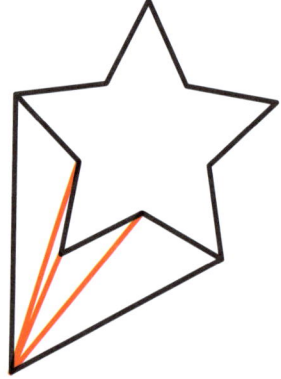

5.

Shade the star light gray. Add some medium gray in the corners.

6.

Shade the diagonal side of the 3D star dark gray.

1.

To begin, lightly draw the guidelines shown in blue.

2.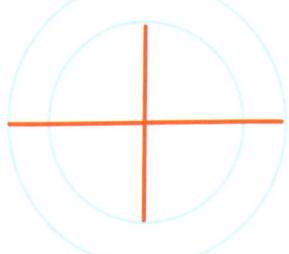

Follow the steps in red to draw a six-pointed star.

3.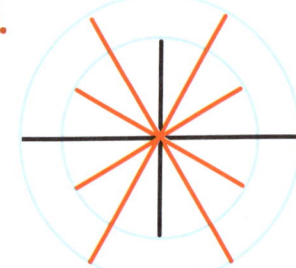

4.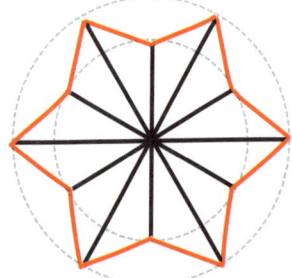

Erase the dashed lines.

5.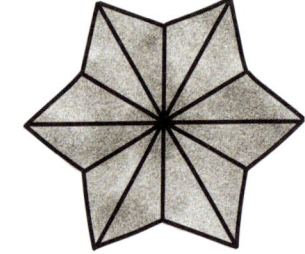

Shade the star medium gray all over.

6.

Shade every other triangle dark gray.

• PRACTICE PAGE •

1. **To begin,** lightly draw as many rectangles as there are letters in your name (shown in blue).

2. **Draw** your name in block letters inside the boxes. Follow the steps in red to draw your 3D name.

3. **Erase** the dashed lines.

Draw a dot below your letters in the middle of your name. Draw a line connecting the bottom left corner of the first letter to the dot. Draw another connecting the bottom right corner of the last letter to the dot.

4. **Continue** connecting the corners of the letters to the dot. Connect all the bottom corners to the dot. If a letter is to the left of the dot, connect the corners on the right side of the letter. If a letter is to the right of the dot, connect the left-side corners.

5. **Draw** a straight line below your name. Erase the diagonal lines below the dot.

6. **Shade** light gray all over.

7. **Shade** the sides of the letters medium gray.

8. **Shade** the sides of each letter that are closest to the center dark gray.

• PRACTICE PAGE •

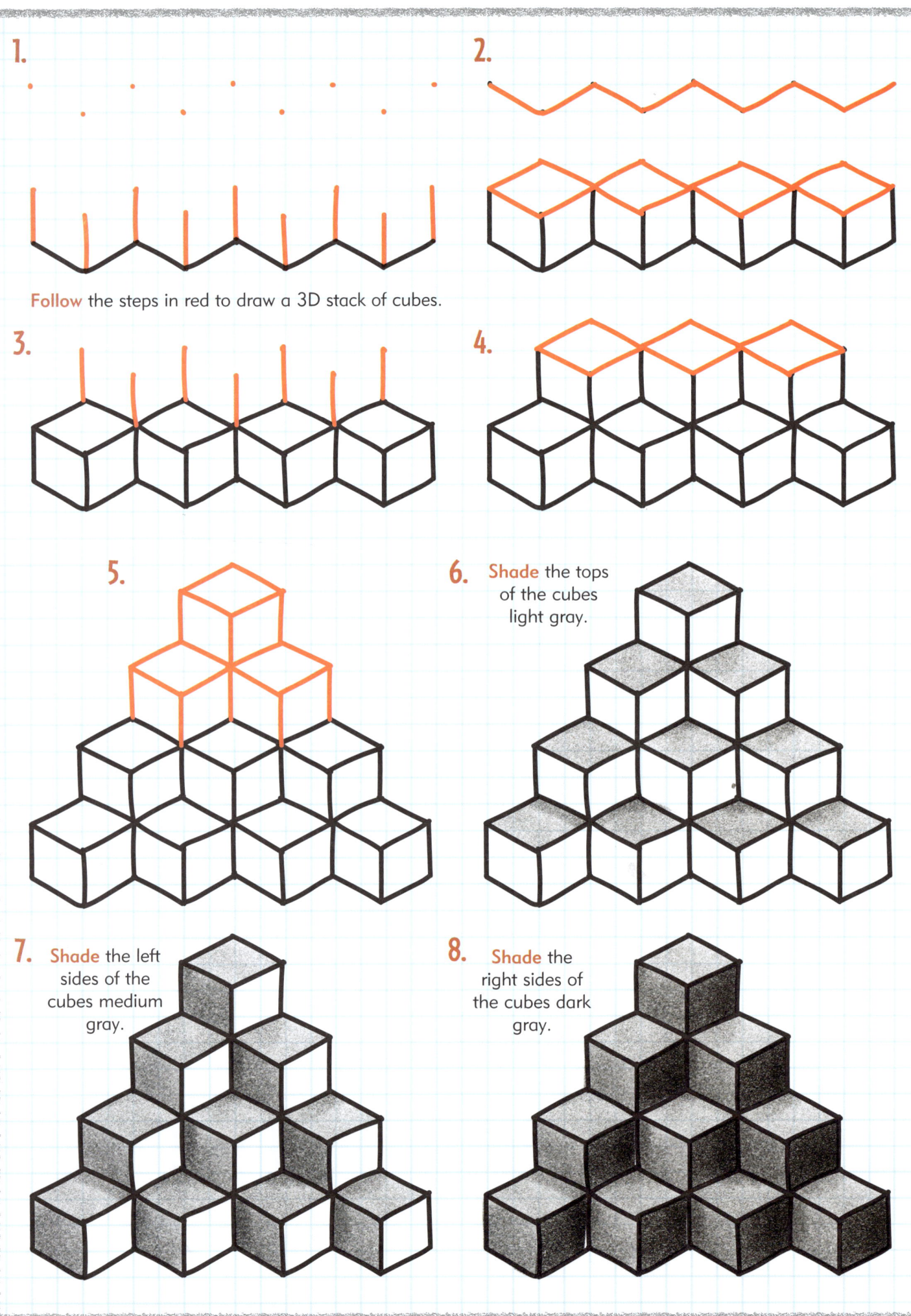

• PRACTICE PAGE •

1.

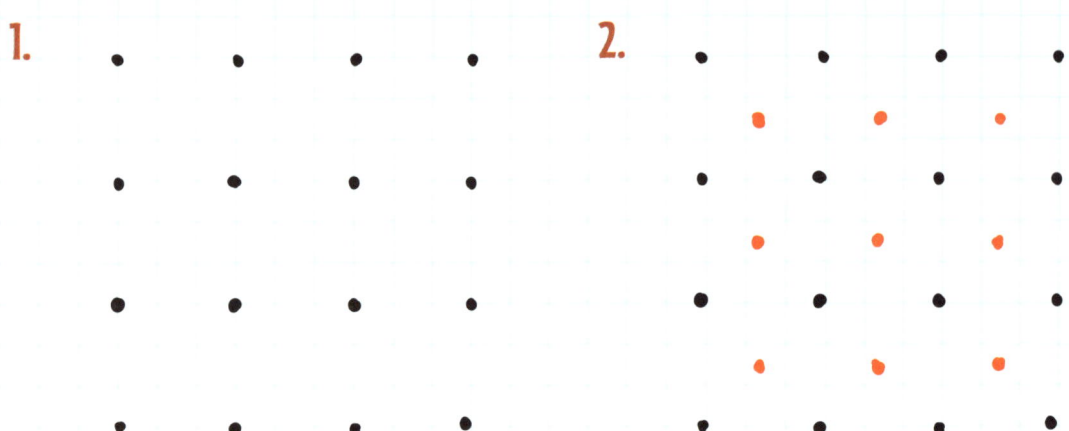

To begin, create a square grid of dots that's four dots high and four dots wide. Try to space your dots as evenly as possible.

2.

In the center of each square of four dots, draw another dot. The dots will guide you as you draw the Celtic knot.

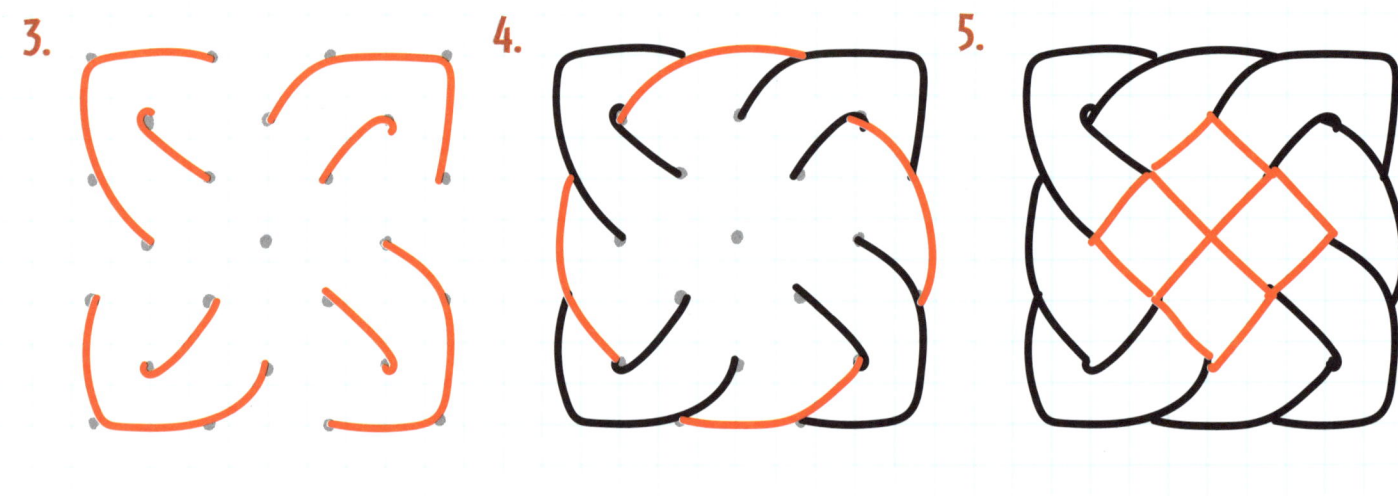

3.

4.

5.

6.

Shade the Celtic knot light gray.

7.

Shade dark gray where the lines of the Celtic knot overlap.

• PRACTICE PAGE •

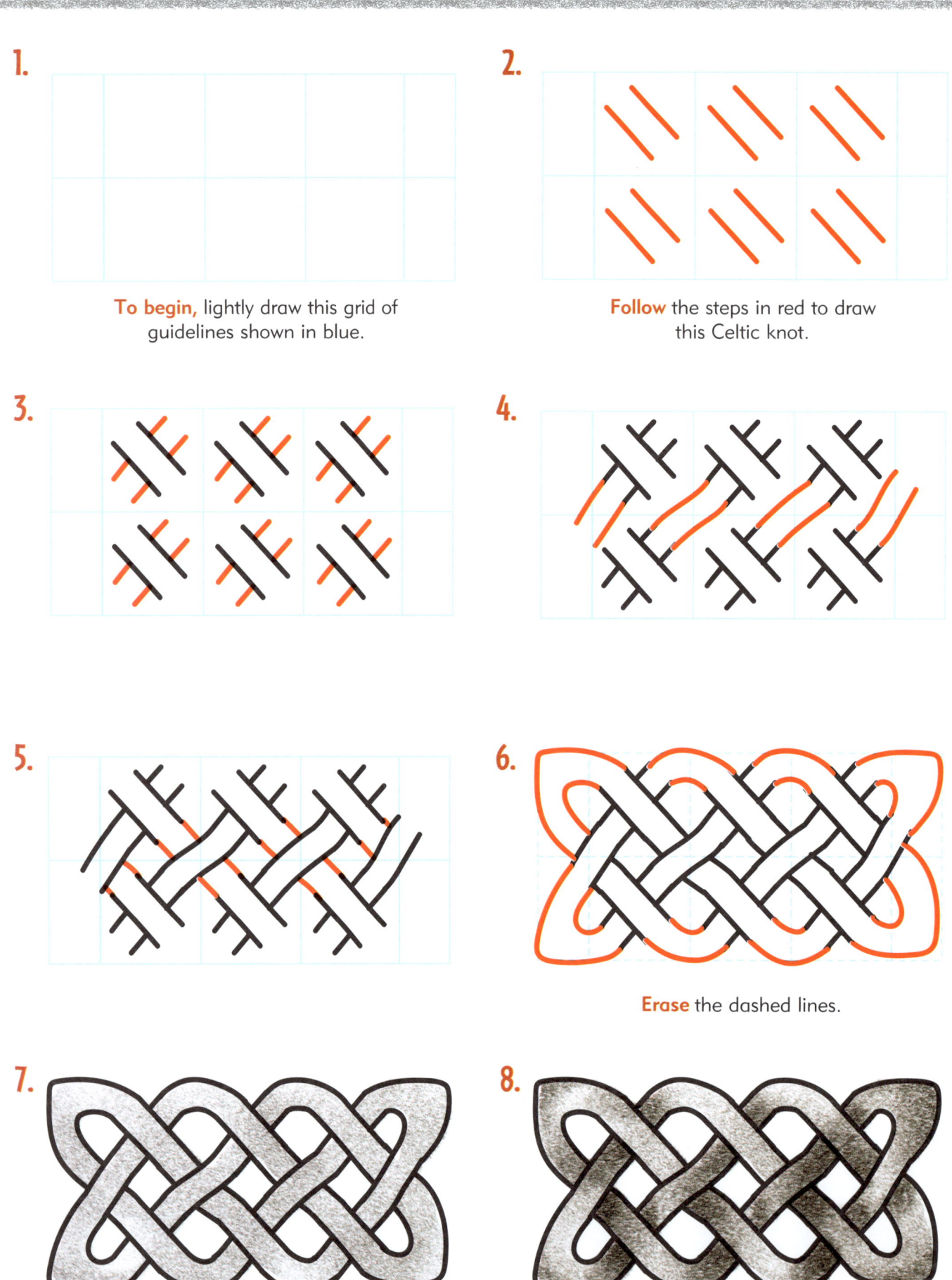

• PRACTICE PAGE •

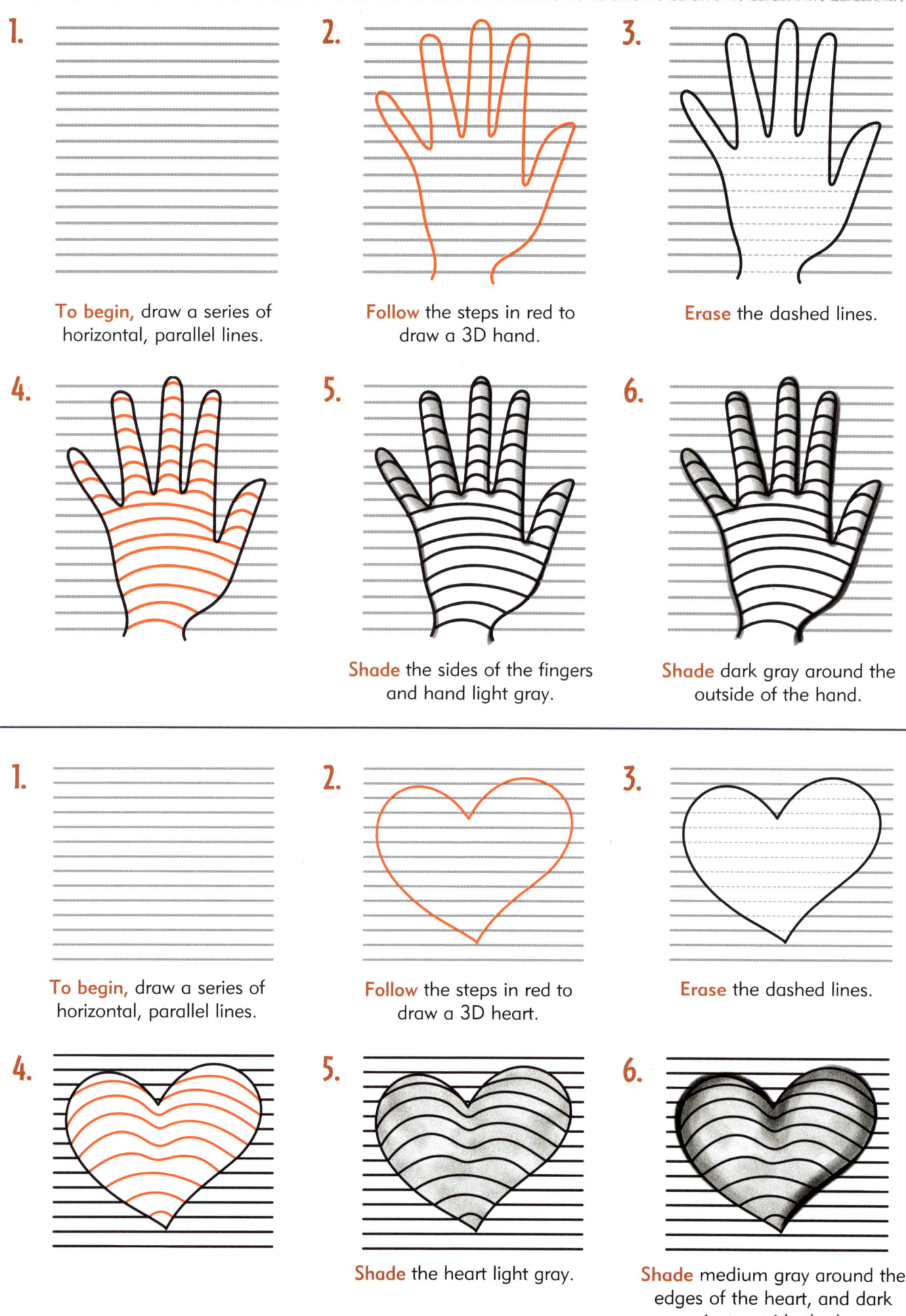

• PRACTICE PAGE •

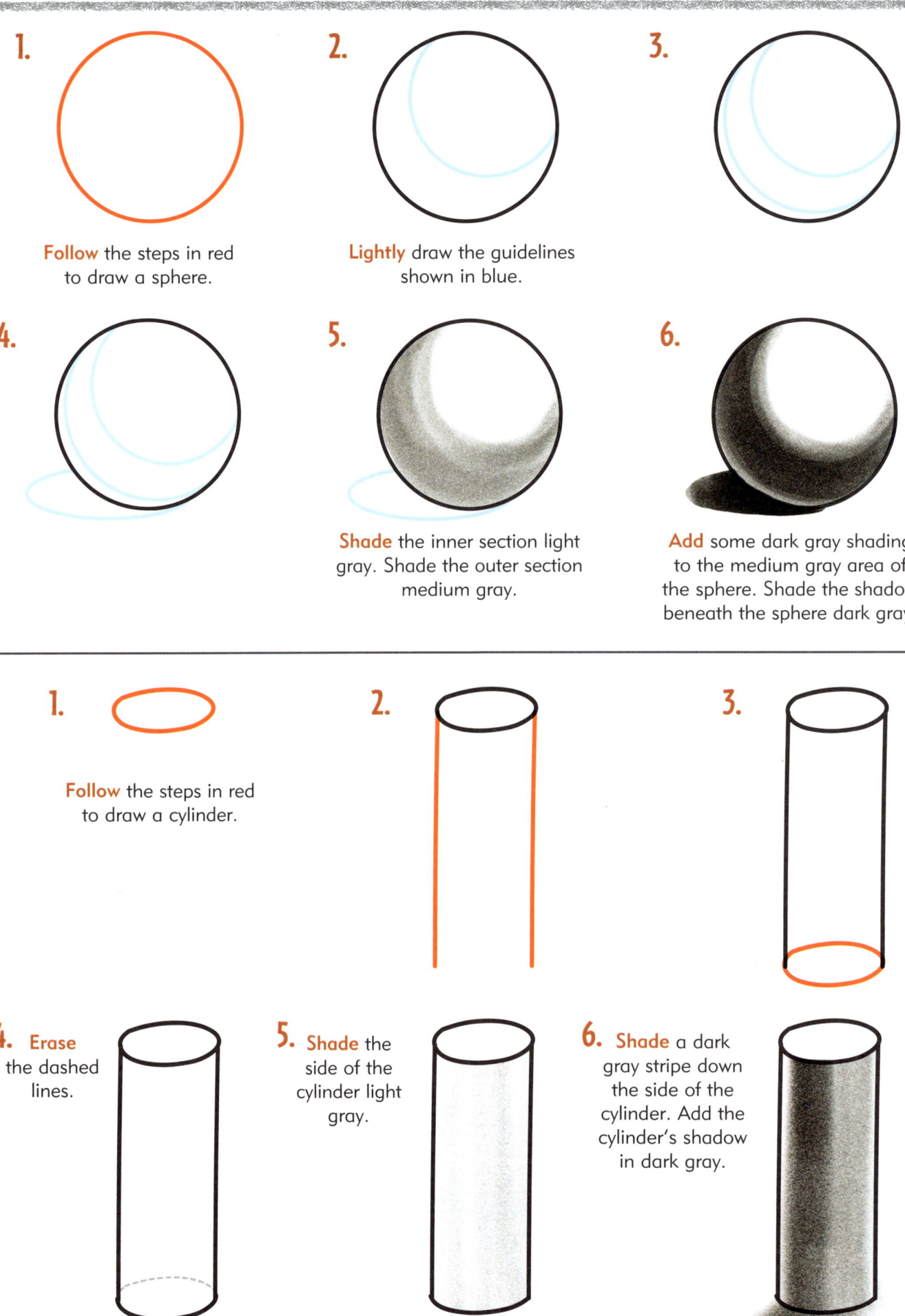

• PRACTICE PAGE •

1.

Follow the steps in red to draw a basketball.

2.

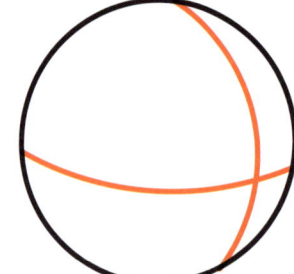

3.

4.

5.

Shade the basketball light gray. Add a little medium gray around the edges.

6.

Add some dark gray around the edges.

1.

Follow the steps in red to draw an impossible oval.

2.

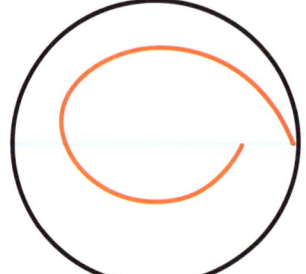

3.

4.

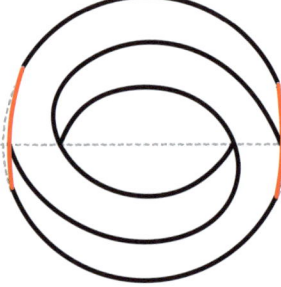

Erase the dashed lines.

5.

Shade medium gray all over.

6.

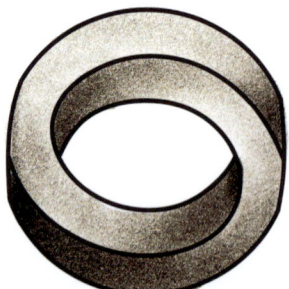

Shade dark gray as shown.

· PRACTICE PAGE ·

1.

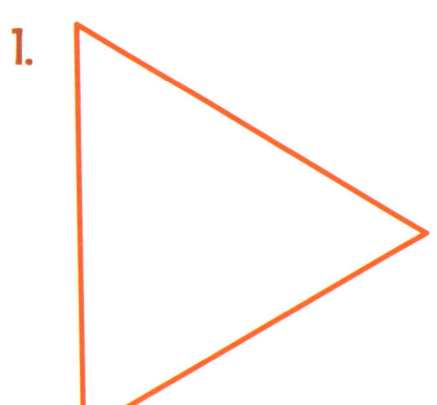

Follow the steps in red to draw an impossible triangle.

2.

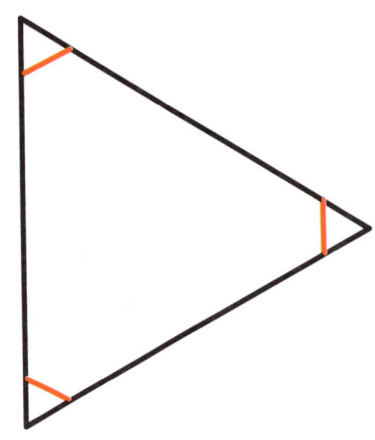

3.

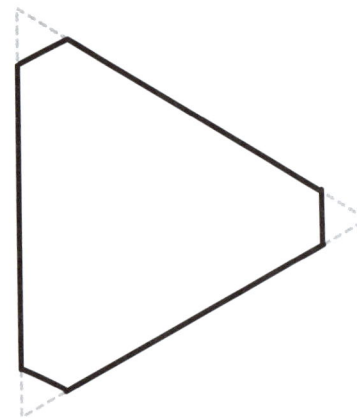

Erase the dashed lines.

4.

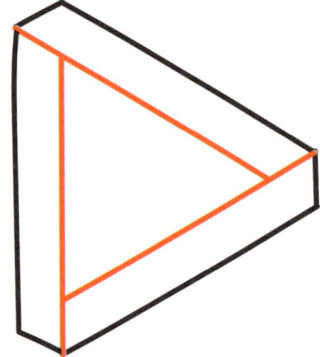

5.

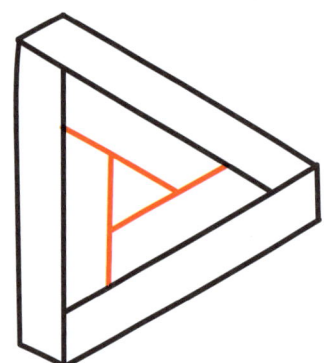

6.

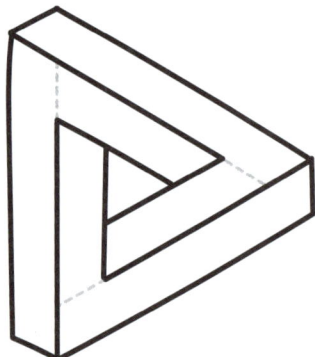

7.

Shade this part light gray.

8.

Shade this part medium gray.

9.

Shade this part dark gray.

• PRACTICE PAGE •

• PRACTICE PAGE •

1.

Follow the steps in red to draw an impossible square.

2.

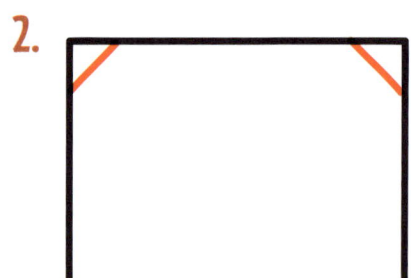

3.

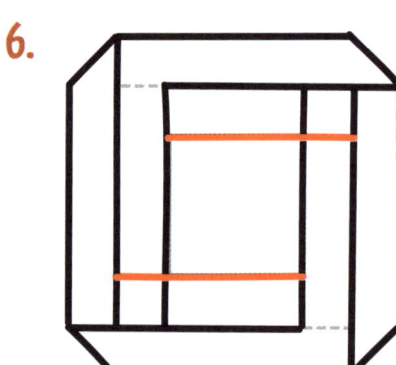

Erase the dashed lines. Lightly draw the guidelines shown in blue.

4.

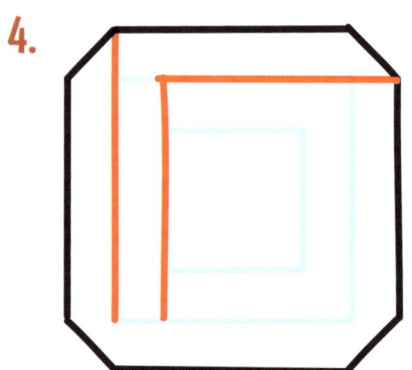

5.

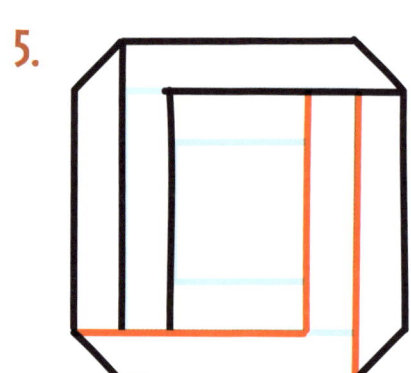

6.

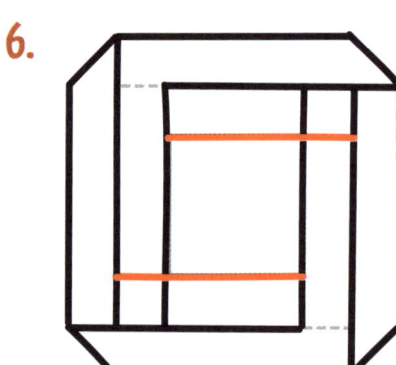

7.

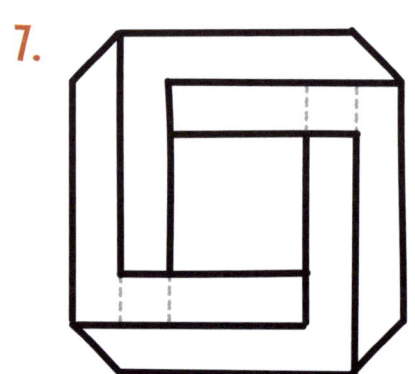

8.

Shade light gray all over.

9.

Shade medium gray and dark gray around the inner corners.

• PRACTICE PAGE •

1.

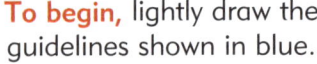

To begin, lightly draw the guidelines shown in blue.

2.

Follow the steps in red to draw this impossible hexagon.

3.

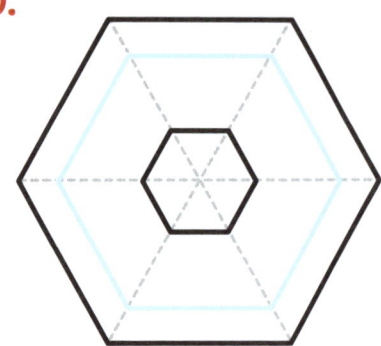

Erase the dashed lines.

4.

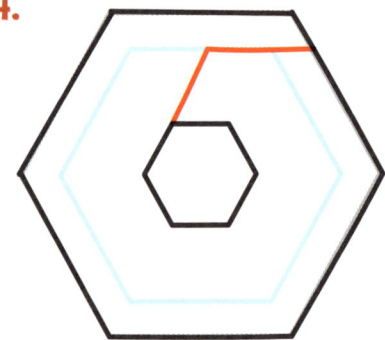

5.

6.

7.

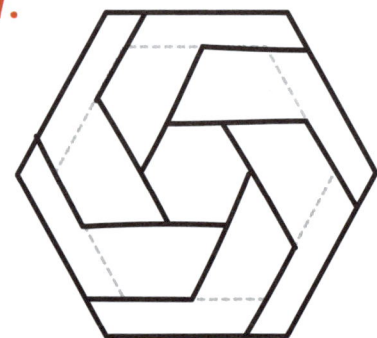

8.

Shade medium gray all over.

9.

Shade dark gray near where the lines overlap.

• PRACTICE PAGE •

1.

Follow the steps in red to draw this swirling square.

2.
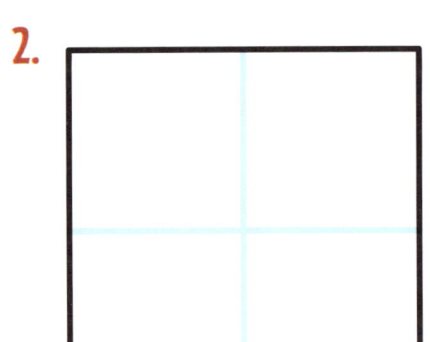
Lightly draw the guidelines shown in blue.

3.
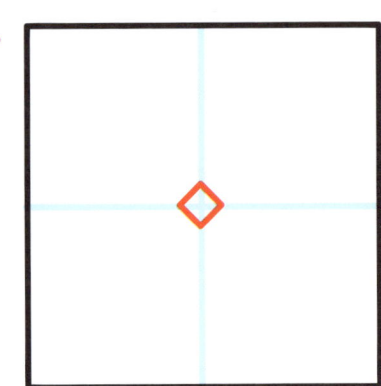

4.
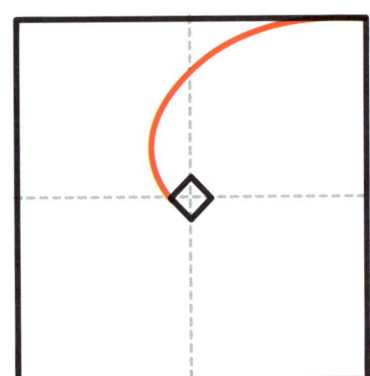
Erase the dashed lines.

5.

6.

7.

8.

Shade every other stripe medium gray.

9.

Shade dark gray in the center. Add a little medium gray along each swirling line.

PRACTICE PAGE

1.

To begin, lightly draw the guidelines shown in blue.

2.

Follow the steps in red to draw this optical illusion hole.

3.

Erase any guidelines still visible.

4. 5. 6.

7.

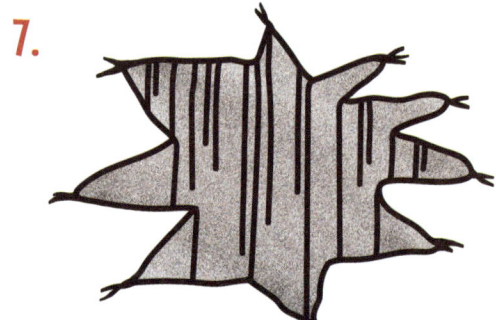

Shade medium gray all over.

8.

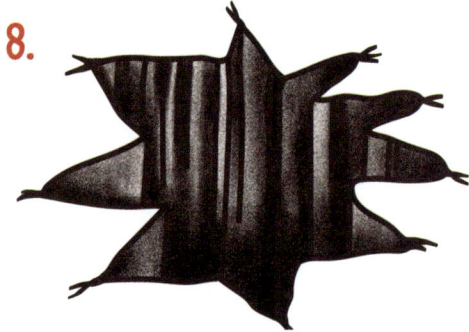

Shade dark gray in corners and along lines, getting darker toward the bottom of the hole.

• PRACTICE PAGE •

1.

To begin, lightly draw the circle shown in blue.

2.

Follow the steps in red to draw this impossible star.

3.

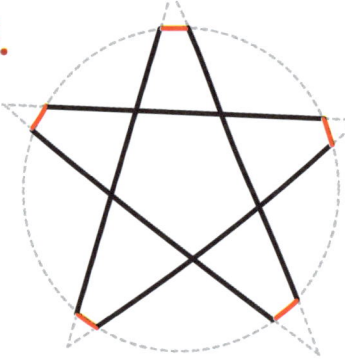

Erase the dashed lines.

4.

5.

6.

7.

8.

9.

10.

11.

12.

13.

Shade these sides medium gray.

14.

Shade these sides dark gray.

• PRACTICE PAGE •

1.

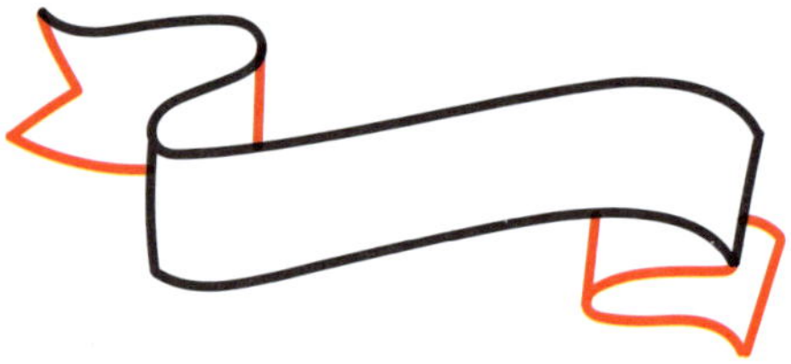

Follow the steps in red to draw this awesome banner.

2.

3.

4.

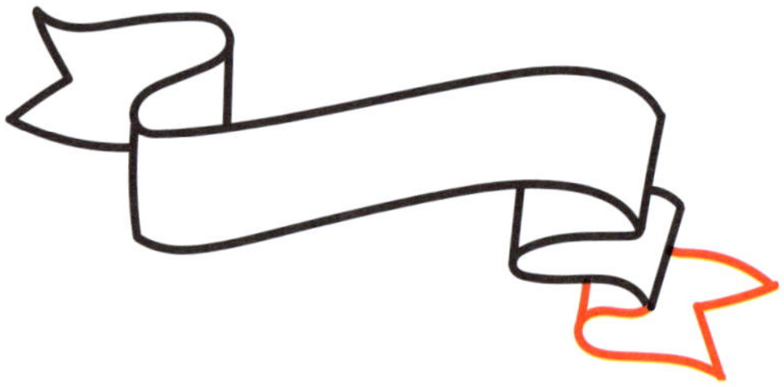

5.

6.  Shade the front sides of the ribbon light gray.

7. Shade the U-shaped back sides of the ribbon medium gray.

1.

Follow the steps in red to draw this banner.

2.

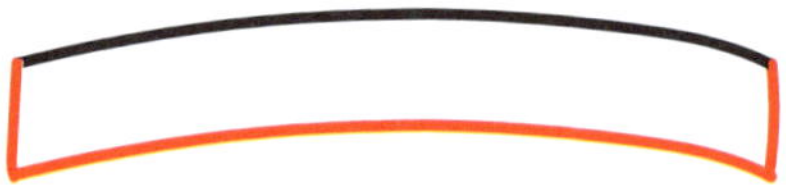

3.

4.

5.

6.  Shade the front sides of the ribbon light gray.

7. Shade the U-shaped back sides of the ribbon dark gray.

• PRACTICE PAGE •

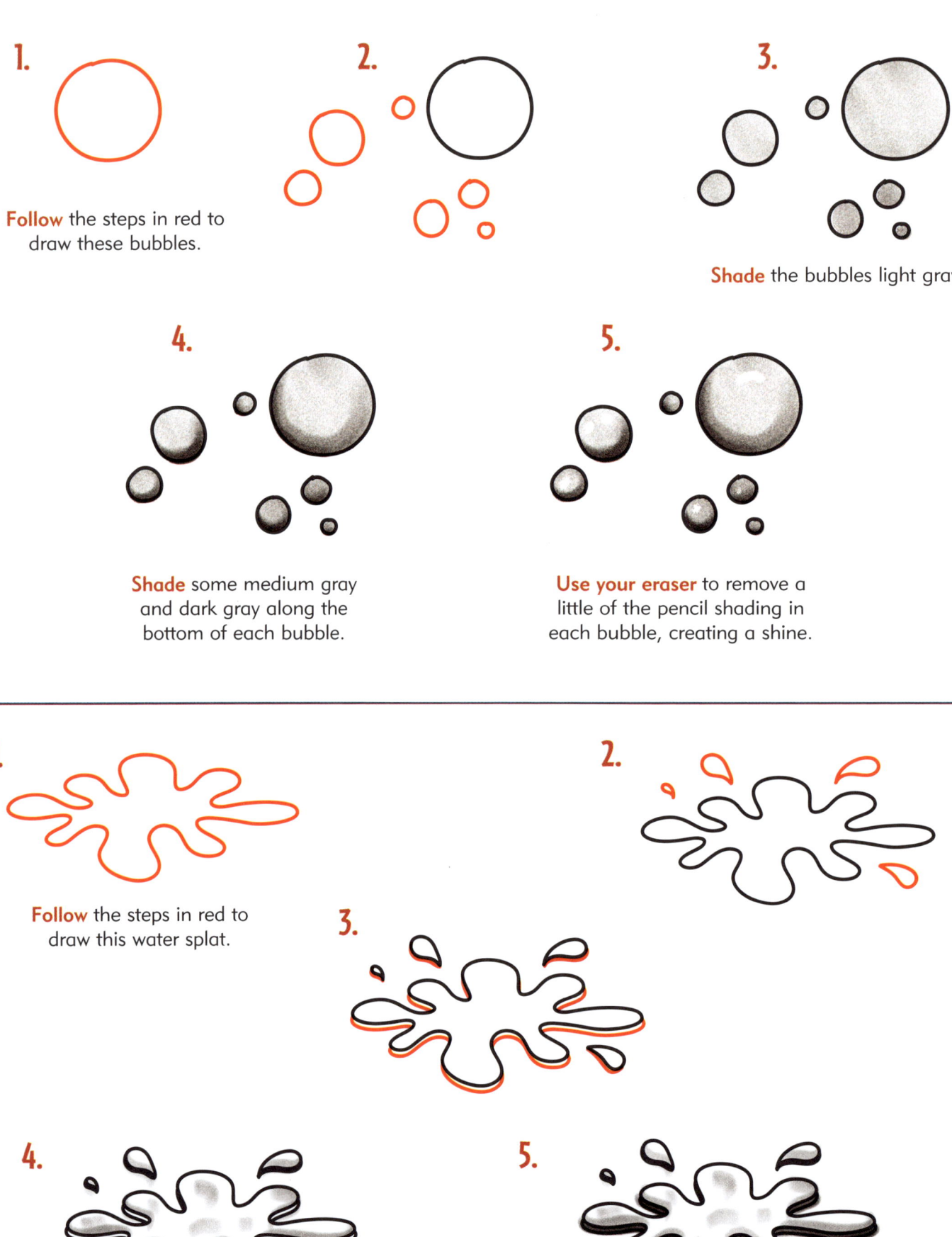

• PRACTICE PAGE •

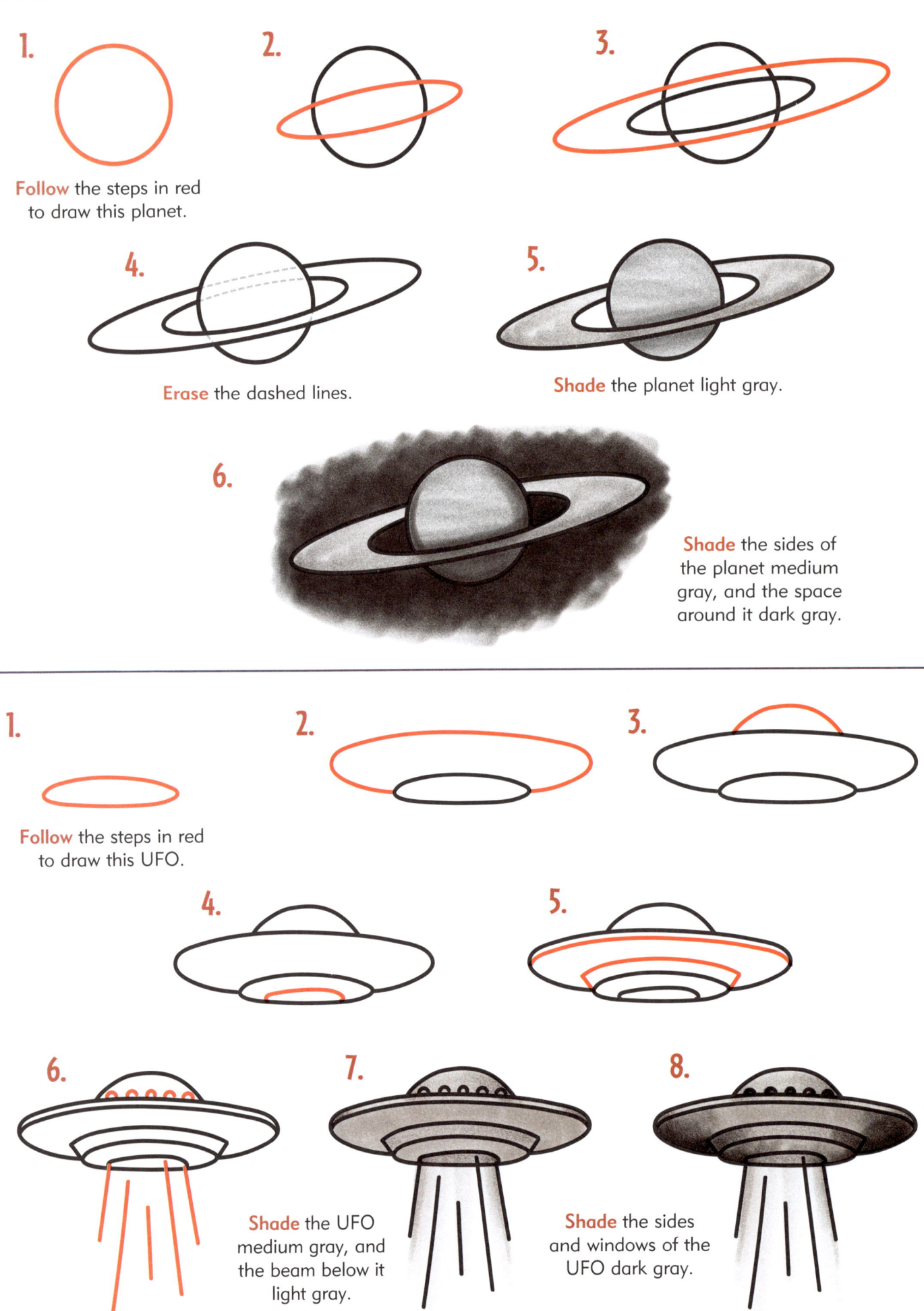

• PRACTICE PAGE •

1.

Follow the steps in red to draw a doghouse.

2.

3.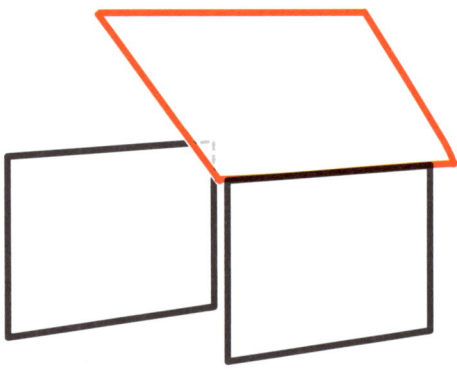

Erase the dashed lines.

4.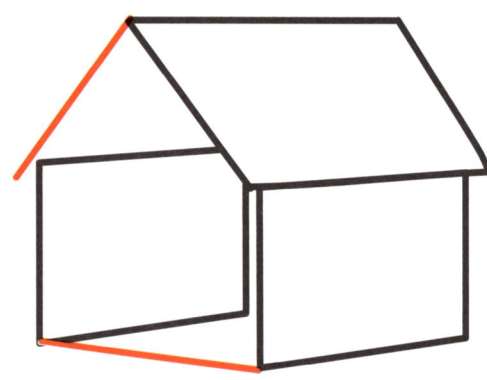

5.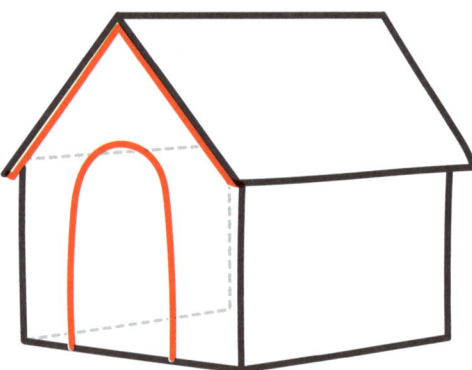

Erase the dashed lines.

6.

7.

Shade the doghouse light gray.

8.

Shade Shade the edges of the doghouse medium gray. Shade the dog dark gray.

• PRACTICE PAGE •

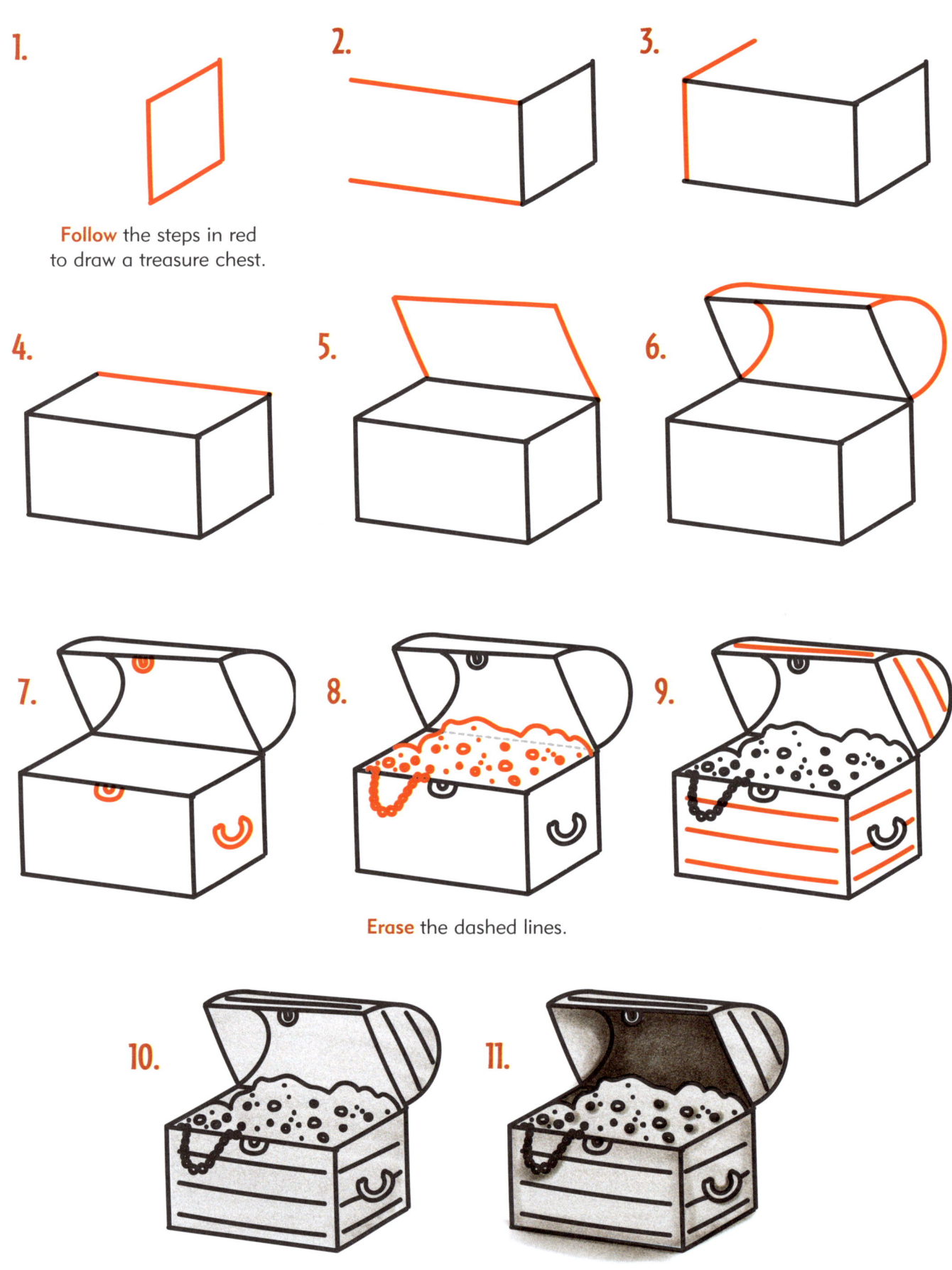

• PRACTICE PAGE •

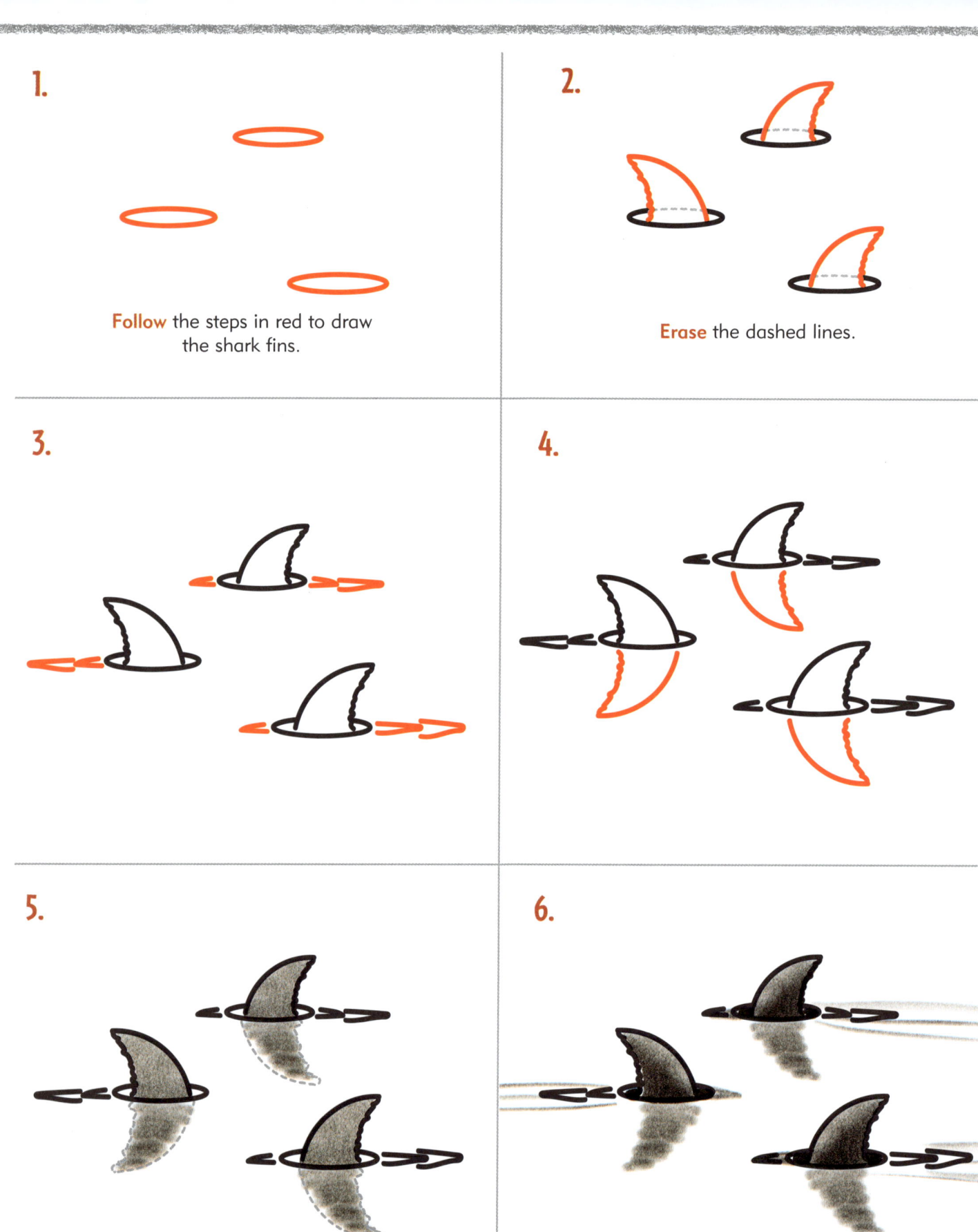

• PRACTICE PAGE •

• PRACTICE PAGE •

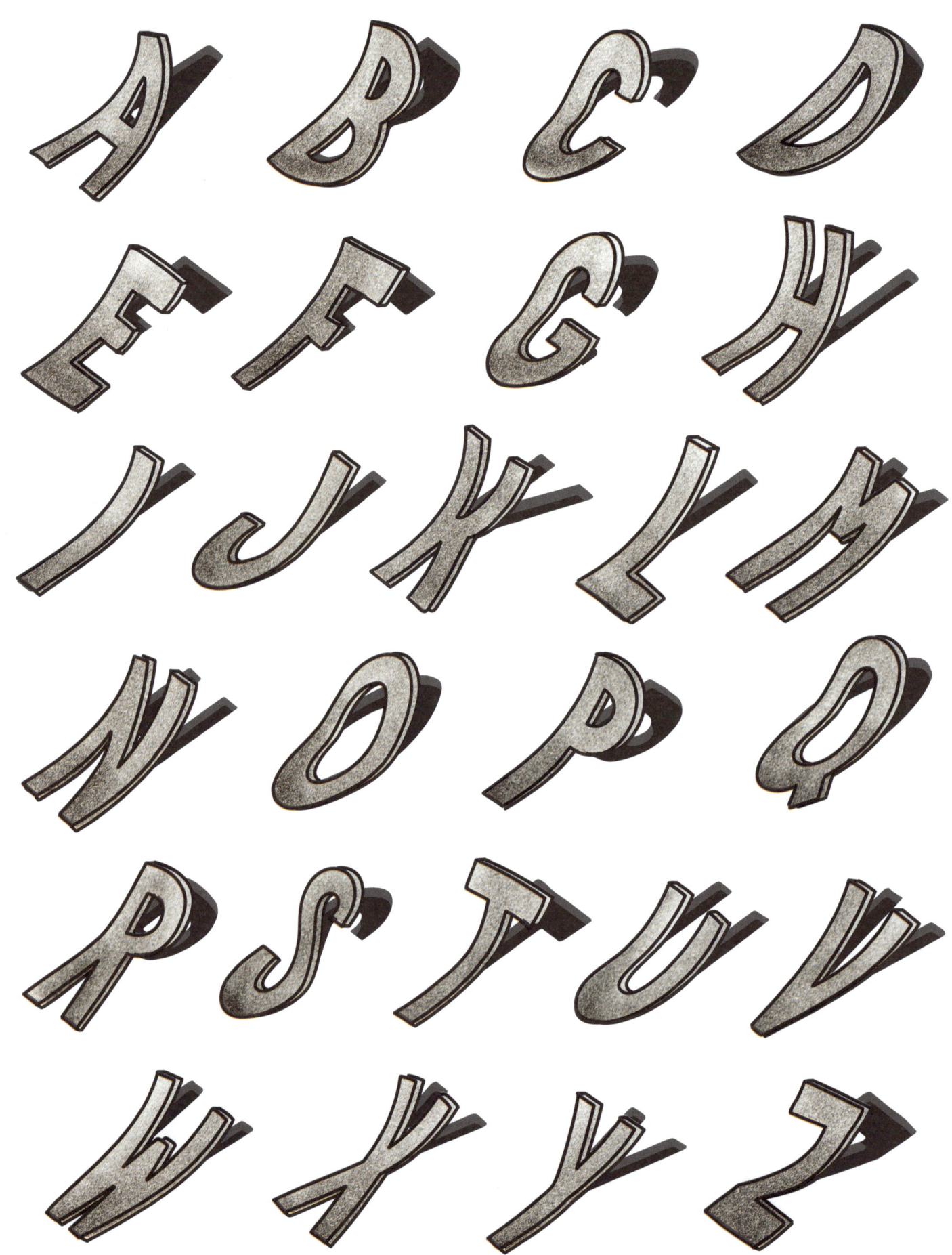

Follow the instructions below to draw the letter **I** in this 3D alphabet, then use the example letters on the previous page to draw your name peeling up from the paper!

1.

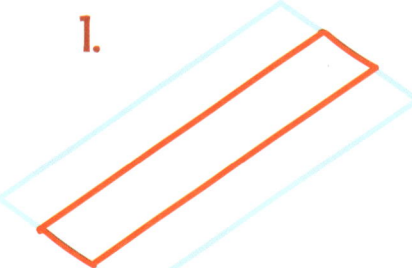

To begin, lightly draw a guideline box for your letter, as shown in blue. Then draw your letter inside the box.

2.

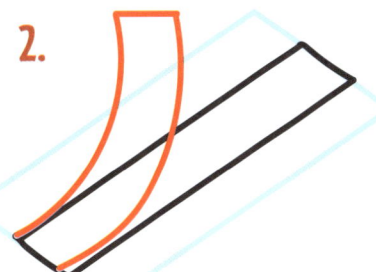

3.

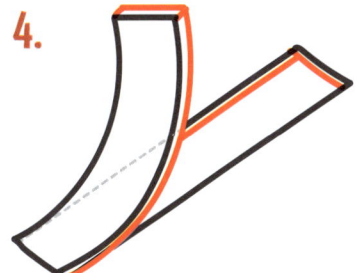

Erase the dashed lines.

4.

5.

Shade the top of the peeled-up letter light gray. Shade the bottom medium gray.

6.

Shade the hole under the letter dark gray. Shade the sides of the letter and the hole medium gray.

• PRACTICE HERE •

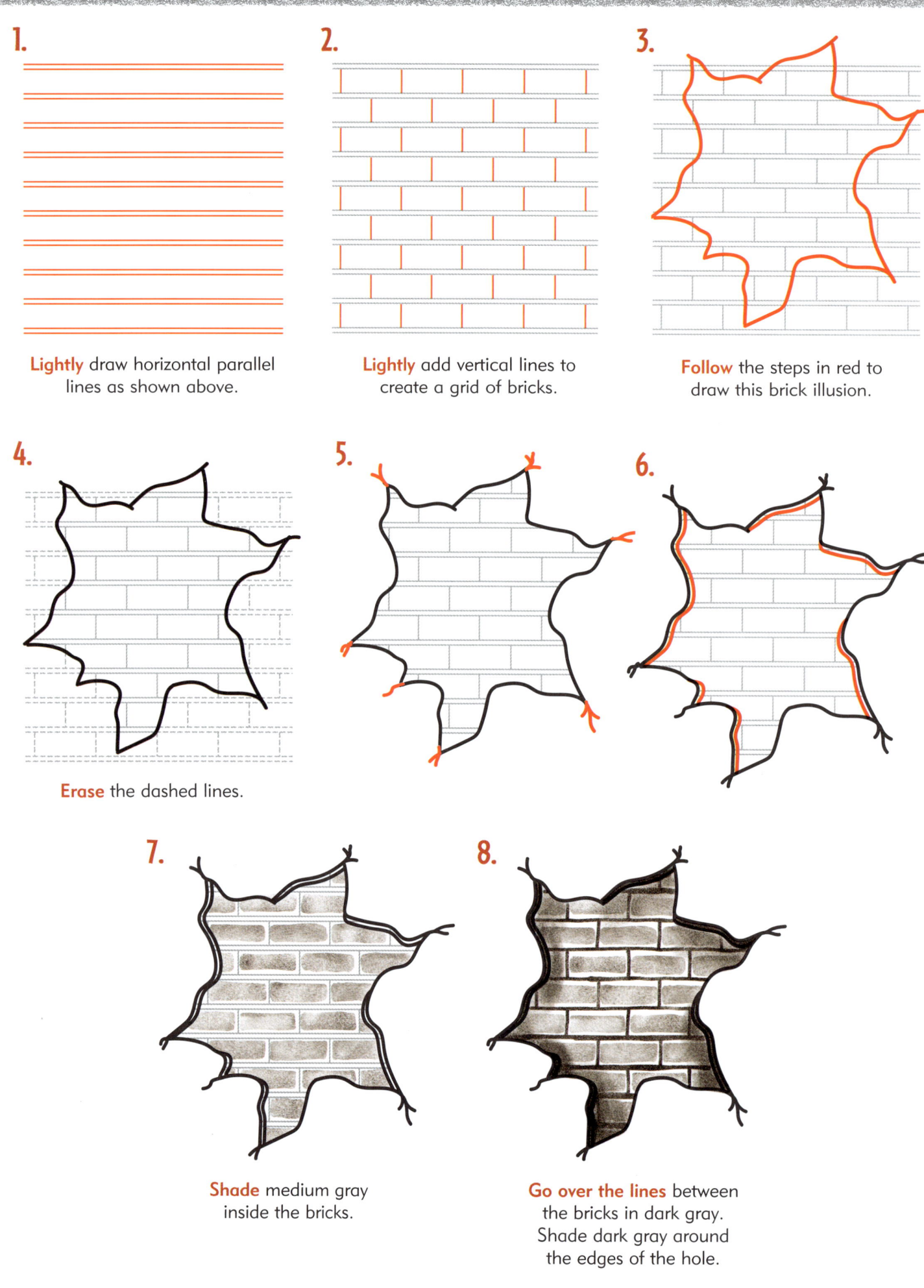

• PRACTICE PAGE •

To create a different brick wall illusion, **follow** steps 1-3 on the previous spread, and then…

1.
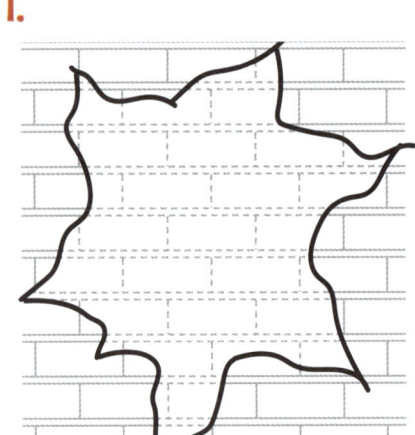
Erase the dashed lines.

2.
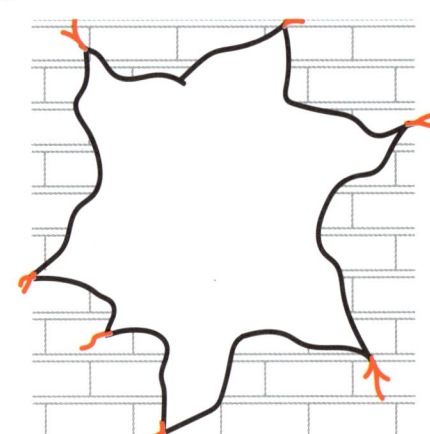

3.
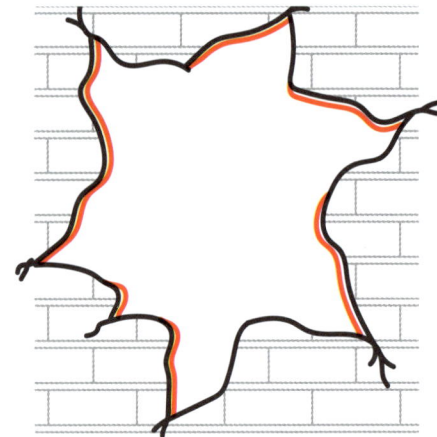

4.
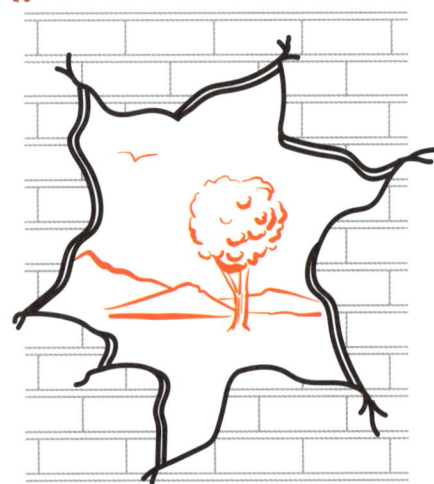

5.

Shade light gray inside the bricks. Shade light and medium gray in the landscape as shown.

6.

Go over the lines between the bricks in dark gray. Shade dark gray around the edges of the hole.

• **PRACTICE HERE** •